THE DECORATIVE ART
OF
ARABIA

THE DECORATIVE ART
OF
ARABIA

PRISSE D'AVENNES

TEXT BY
JULES BOURGOIN

FOREWORD BY
CHARLES NEWTON
ASSISTANT CURATOR
DEPARTMENT OF DESIGN, PRINTS AND DRAWINGS
VICTORIA AND ALBERT MUSEUM
LONDON

STUDIO EDITIONS

LONDON

Published by Studio Editions
an imprint of Bestseller Publications Ltd.
Princess House, 50 Eastcastle Street
London W1N 7AP
ENGLAND

The Decorative Art of Arabia
contains a selection of plates from
*L'Art Arabe d'après les monuments du Kaire
depuis le VIIe siècle jusqu'à la fin du XVIIIe siècle*
by Achille-Constant-Théodore-Émile Prisse d'Avennes
Vve. A. Morel et Cie.
Libraires-Éditeurs
13 rue Bonaparte
Paris
1869–1877

and an edited section of the text from
Les Arts Arabes et le Trait Général de l'Art Arabe
by Jules Bourgoin
Vve. A. Morel et Cie.
Libraires-Éditeurs
13 rue Bonaparte
Paris
1873

ISBN 1 85170 189 3

Printed in Hong Kong

FOREWORD

When Napoleon invaded Egypt in 1798, he took with him a fully-equipped scientific task force of *Savants*, who intended to make the most of the opportunities for gathering knowledge afforded them by right of conquest. Although Napoleon's dreams of an Eastern empire foundered when Nelson burnt the French fleet at Aboukir, the detailed surveys of ancient and modern Egypt that these experts initiated have continued to the present day.

The first fruits of the *Savants'* labours, the 23 volumes of text and plates entitled *Description de l'Egypte*, 1809–20, had to be illustrated in the eighteenth century manner with engraving and etching in black and white. Yet at that moment in 1798 when Napoleon was addressing his troops at the foot of the Pyramids, in Germany the inventor Senefelder was developing the completely new process of print making, now called lithography. This was to revolutionize the reproduction of paintings and drawings, so that, by 1867, when Prisse d'Avennes published the first volumes of *L'Art Arabe*, colour lithography had not only supplanted older forms of illustration but had reached new heights of technical perfection.

Artist, writer, linguist, archaeologist, traveller and engineer, Achille-Constant-Théodore-Émile Prisse d'Avennes, 1807–1879, was among the second wave of *Savants* that took up residence in Egypt. He had studied at Chalons-sur-Marne, and after early adventures in the Greek War of Independence and travel in Palestine and India, took employment in 1829 as a military adviser and engineer in the service of Mohammed Ali, the ruler of Egypt.

Prisse resigned in 1836 and travelled extensively in the near East as a Muslim. Based at Luxor he explored Upper and Lower Egypt. In 1843 he secretly removed and shipped to France the *King List* from the Temple of Amun, and he received the Legion of Honour in 1845. He published various books and scholarly publications, including *Les Monuments Egyptiens*, 1847, and *L'Histoire de l'Art Egyptien . . .* , 1858–77.

The magnificent plates in our book are reproduced from his *L'Art Arabe d'après les monuments du Kaire depuis le VIIe siècle jusqu'a la fin du XVIIIe siècle,* published 1869–77. Ancient Egypt had by then been extensively illustrated, but the splendours of

[5]

Islamic Egypt, dating from the time of the conquest by the Arabs in the seventh century, the usurpation of the Mamelukes in the thirteenth and the invasion of the Ottomans in the sixteenth century, were fast disappearing before the modernization enforced by Mohammed Ali and his successors. So Prisse's three volumes of 200 plates and one volume of text illustrating mosques, *The Koran*, artifacts, monuments and houses of the Arabs and their Mameluke usurpers, came not a moment too soon.

Many other artists, architects and writers were fascinated by the wealth of unfamiliar pattern and the brilliant abstract and geometrical designs. The most famous French architect, designer and restorer of nineteenth century Gothic, Viollet-le-Duc wrote the preface to a rival work about Egypt, *Les Arts Arabes et le Trait Général de l'Art Arabe*, 1873, by the architect Jules Bourgoin, part of whose text is translated and reprinted here.

This publication was significant because Bourgoin, through his desire to bring to a wider public the glories of Islamic design, took his analytic approach much further than had his predecessors, Pascal Coste and Prisse d'Avennes.

Coste, although an extraordinary talented draftsman, offered little comment or analyses of what he saw, and was content to identify briefly what he illustrated. Prisse d'Avennes, too, still belonged to that earlier generation of travellers and archaeolgists who elegantly and simply recorded what they found and tried to put it into its historical context.

When Bourgoin persuaded Viollet-le-Duc to write a preface for him, it was part of a deliberate strategy as well as a ploy to increase sales. Viollet-le-Duc was also a design theorist, so that simply to present Islamic patterns with no attempt at analysis would have been unthinkable, especially as the exercise was partly propagandist, intended to promote the adoption of a systematic eclecticism in design. This entailed the borrowing and amalgamation of historic styles and repertoires to form a new, coherent and viable modern style in which to build and decorate.

Thus Viollet-le-Duc and Jules Bourgoin wished to influence their fellow architects and designers, providing both a book of patterns and a kind of cultural analysis upon which to ground their theories.

Behind European decorative art of the nineteenth century there was a large amount of theory, instilled by various academics, critics and other arbiters of taste; yet for Islamic art there were no similar treatises in Arabic on how things ought to look, or not in any form that a European could readily assimilate. There was only the work itself. The artisans of Egypt were still in that happy medieval state where there was no division between art and craft, and although there were many Islamic artists and designers of genius whose names are known, somehow the concept of the artist as hero isolated

[6]

from his fellows was a Western one not then found in Islam. Designers learnt their skills in workshops, and design had evolved naturally, without self-consciousness.

The intricate geometrical patterns, the interlace of astonishing complexity were created with a maximum of skill and the minimum of equipment and theory. New patterns were essentially variants of older ones, and a straight-edge and dividers were the only instruments used to lay out the ground.

As Bourgoin emphasizes, somehow the Islamic artists reflected the underlying geometric structure of organic things in their patterns, but they achieved this intuitively, not through experimental science or a formal study of geometry. Although built up from simple elements, the number of possible designs is infinite, but only through the study of existing patterns can new patterns be made.

Charles Newton
August 1988

PREFACE
E. Viollet-le-Duc
to Jules Bourgoin's *Les Arts Arabes*

It would be difficult to say exactly when elementary geometry was first applied to decorative composition. In the earliest Egyptian monuments we can find right angles and circle segments both painted and sculpted; geometric figures are also to be found in the ornamentation of monuments in India, Syria and Asia Minor well before the Islamic invasion. It would be too short-sighted to consider this type of ornamentation as a wholly 'Arabic' phenomenon. Besides which, from the point of view of art history, who are the Arabs? Do they exist? Did they initiate or simply develop? Did they bring something which really belonged to them into the countries they conquered? I believe that the denomination 'Arabic art' is rather equivocal and, historically speaking, vague in the extreme. But let us not quibble over words. We are obliged to designate the term Arabic art to art as manifested in the territories and races conquered in the name of Islam from Asia to Spain, and so be it. This is an art which precludes, at least in a general sense, any representation of animate beings, thus limiting its decorative conception to forms borrowed from geometry and some from flora, this itself being subject to the laws of geometry. This tendency is particularly in evidence among semitic peoples, especially with the arrival of Islam. Here, where races are mixed, ornamentation is subject to diverse influences; representations borrowed from organic nature are assimilated with purely geometric combinations. This is found to be true in Persia, Sicily, and Arab-influenced Spain.

Since the beginning of the fourth century AD, and thus before the invasion of the conquering Arab peoples, Christian monuments in central Syria already displayed this kind of ornament composed of geometric figures which we call interlace, and with very few exceptions these ornaments bear no relation to animal imagery. Furthermore, as these buildings in central Syria owe their construction to the thoroughly semiticized Greek colonists, there can be no possibility of considering this geometric interlace as being exclusively Arabic in origin. Besides which, as we have already noted, long before the advent of Christianity, Ionian and Syrian edifices provide evidence of geometric interlace taking the form of flat decoration grooved into the stone as in a tapestry; in no way

[8]

were the Arabs involved in these creations.

Unfortunately, nothing remains of the Egyptian monuments of the Alexandrian period; the armies of Omar destroyed the monuments of the Lower Nile along with the libraries; and if his Lieutenant Amrou constructed mosques we can presume that these were built by the vanquished rather that the conquering soldiers, and that their decoration would have been a simple reproduction of the style adopted before the conquest with its total prohibition on the reproduction of human or animal figures. The geometric interlace tradition would therefore appear to belong to the Greek decadent schools, and certainly not to the populations or, rather, tribes scattered along the coast of the Red Sea and the Persian Gulf. It is scarcely likely that the armies of Omar and his successors took artists along with them with the intention of imposing an architectural style on the conquered country. A man of genius can assemble, organize and instruct an army in a matter of months, but to establish a school of art takes centuries and the human will alone is insufficient to form and develop it.

Whatever the origin of this ornamentation we choose to call Arabic, it has a distinct character. In its general aspect it represents what we call in architecture a 'tapestry', that is to say a flat, decorated surface with fairly even projections and distributions, closer to engraving or chasings than to sculpture, and recalling in its execution, decoration of the buildings of ancient Egypt. This kind of decoration is to be found in Indian monuments of the fifth and sixth centuries BC, but this is also the ornamentation of round-relief sculpture and exaggerated projections. So it is that monuments in India and the kingdom of Siam in the wonderful Buddhist period are adorned with not only flat-relief ornamentation resembling embossed fabric but also sweeping projections whose power and effect eclipse anything in even the finest European architecture. Nothing of the like is to be found in so-called Arabic ornamentation, which never exceeds a minimum of embossing. These artists of the Orient, then, adhering strictly to this process either according to tradition or, more often, submitting to policies imposed by their conquerors, were singularly restricted in the matter of composition. We have said that these artists were subject to certain policies in the field of creativity imposed on them by their new masters; this is because, since time immemorial, the conquering Arabs had lived in tents, as had most semitic peoples. Their only luxuries were arms and fabrics. For them, like the Jews of the primitive period, the monument was the tent, covered with precious materials; they could accustom themselves to these indented surfaces, resplendent with projections and sculptures, which they were to encounter travelling along a path strewn with reminders of the Greek and Roman civilizations. These statues, the 'bas-reliefs', the projected friezes

[9]

bearing great foliated scrolls intermixed with human and animal figures, must have appeared to the Arabs as monstrous manifestations of the warped imagination of pantheism. We should admit, then, that the Alexandrian school had not itself adopted the tapestry style of decoration before the Arab invasion; there is every reason to believe that the invaders imposed the adoption of this style, the only style which man could permit himself in the face of the one and only God, whose works are not to be imitated by his creation.

Unable to bring to their decorations the world of everyday objects, the image of man, animals or even plants, the artists had but one door open to them – geometry – an abstraction – at least for the doctors of Islam, who saw no evidence in this science of the 'thing created', nor most probably did they see any universal order, a general law to which all created things must submit. It is not on the philosophical side that the semitic mind shines brightest, and they were certainly unaware that to leave geometry in the hands of the artist to compose their decorations was to provide him with the creative tool *par excellence*; the principle on which the whole of creation in the material order depends; but let us not accuse Islamics of too many contradictions; they could quite easily defend themselves I am sure.

Those of us who have tried to draw some of these Arab ornamentations we refer to as interlace will know that one is initially seized by a kind of vertigo in face of the tangle of straight and curved lines which combine to form a harmonious, concrete whole, but in which the combination of elements seems to defy analysis. These drawings bring to mind the kind of network of tracery produced when sections of vegetal or animal organs are placed under the microscope. But if we proceed by the analytical method, if we first trace certain lines which appear to be controlling the system, we realize that the principle of these complex compositions is one of perfect simplicity.

Graphic arts have their own philosophy; we must understand how to go deeper than what is simply apparent in form; we must analyse the creative principles: this is the only method which will enable us, in turn, to be creative.

E. Viollet-Le-Duc
1873

INTRODUCTION
Jules Bourgoin

The general observations on Islamic art that follow are necessarily incomplete because in order to give a view of the totality of this art we would have to collect enough material from all the territories which once constituted the vast Arab empire; we would have to understand the essential theoretical bases and the historical links between diverse influences which combined to charge its brilliant awakening. We have to admit that we are far from being able to do this; the aesthetic of Islamic art is insufficiently developed. For the moment the reader must be content with a number of general guidelines indicating the route we have chosen and the goal we are pursuing.

First, a word about what we know of Oriental art to establish what ideas we already have about it and what any new or previously unpublished documents reveal.

Ideas brought to mind by the narratives of poets or the descriptions of travellers, what we know of Moorish art in Spain, the designs and mouldings of the Alhambra, a thousand little objects which are the focus of so much avid contemporary curiosity; this represents the image of the modern Orient with which we content ourselves. Viewed in this way, a truer or more developed understanding of the Muslim countries would add little to this received idea which, being complete in itself, is at least equal to the imagination.

This kind of superficial curiosity aroused by the purely superficial is less than demanding. Romanticism awoke all manner of poetic fancies and, scattering them in the imagination, centred our attention on Spain and created an exaggerated appetite for the Moorish monuments the Arabs built there.

The descriptive poets themselves were satisfied with relatively little, and their poetry is inconsequential; but the same is not true of art. We were readily seduced by the novelty of forms and the slightly gaudy decoration in Moorish art. We paid attention to it and with each successive discovery, interest awakening, we began to gather together from drawings and mouldings material to furnish our decorative arts with motifs drawn from entirely new forms. Today, we can recognize the value of this importation, still evident in the famous oriental style.

If the clumsy and ill-considered exploitation of these new-found sources were our only cause of regret, we should have little to complain about: Moorish decoration and Turkish cafés are scarcely to everyone's taste nor are they genuinely admired. Moorish ornamentation has been applied much in the same way as were Assyrian and Egyptian motifs, whose extremely characterized nature yields unreadily to modern composition and whose use betrays poor taste and paucity of invention on the part of the artists.

But there is a more serious side: the whole occidental section of the vast Muslim empire, that is to say Spain and its annexes – Morocco, Algeria, Tunisia and Sicily – has provided practically the entirety of our understanding of Arab civilization. The focus of attention on the monuments in these various countries and particularly on those in Spain has left us with a materialistic impression, physical so to speak, which is extremely difficult to exorcize. It is from this impression that we have formed an idea (such as it is) of Arabic art. It follows, therefore, that any analogous materials originating in the Oriental regions will be appreciated in terms of this same idea, that they will be seen as it were, through an image of the Alhambra. It is important to take this disadvantage into account.

Few people have had the privilege of contemplating the monuments of the Orient and it is therefore extremely difficult to give a complete idea. Drawings and a few detailed explanations can but imperfectly convey the true, complete sensation perceived by the eye. Thus it is essential that the reader endeavours to see beyond the image, and arrives at a conception of things as they are in reality, rather than in representation.

If we pay some attention to the whole, if we eschew all superficial examinations, if we observe and compare with all due attention these examples of Arabic art, we will be obliged to recognize a considerable difference between the Moorish art of Spain and the Arabic art of Egypt and Syria; and by induction, we will discover that there may be many more aspects of this Oriental art at large in the vast Muslim empire. We should go even further and admit that what we know about this art up to the present amounts to very little, and that it is necessary, at least in the short term, to forget about the Moorish style which, being the only one we know, has provided an inaccurate perspective on Arabic art as a whole.

For any understanding of Arabic art is it necessary to follow and to study the growth of the Arab conquest throughout the world, that is to say in every territory of this vast region of the planet extending from India to southern Europe and including a major part of Persia, India, western Asia, Turkey, Spain and its annexes.

With the information available to us today it is difficult to define the precise role played by the Arab race in this blossoming of the arts in the Orient. The Arab conquest engulfed so many different peoples of such diverse racial origins, it took root in so many diverse regions in which had previously flourished the colossal civilizations of India, Assyria, Persia and of Greco-Roman antiquity, that it is difficult to know how much influence should be attributed to the conquest and how much is residual to the vanquished countries. However, we should notice that the monumental constructions erected since the advent of Islam are in perfect correlation with the monuments surviving from previous civilizations.

All the conquering Arabs overrunning the world to the rallying cry of the Prophet, and for eight centuries imposing their activity on the planet, were in no way barbarians; they knew a lot about the world around them and, conquerors or conquered, they shared that particular tempering of spirit which so profoundly distinguishes the Asiatic from the European; they shared the same or, at least analogous principles. The conquest was also very rapid, extending within only a few centuries from the Far East to the south of Europe.

Arabic art is essentially decorative and deals in surfaces; but where monuments had been built using substantially large basic materials, Arab civilizations employed the same means. This is what happened in India, Egypt and western Asia. In Persia on the other hand, where architecture consisted principally of revetment, Persian Islamic art reveals the use of small-scale materials such as bricks, faced with plaster or faïence. In Spain and in Africa Moorish architecture is all of one piece and considerably lacks – a point which is important to note – the wealth of architectural construction inherent in most other systems. Moorish architecture is an architecture of decoration, which renders it inferior, and this is why we should not judge the art of the Orient in terms of what we understand about Moorish or African countries.

From all this, we can begin to understand the importance of the milieu. If one considers the paucity of artistic activity among the original semitic or 'semiticized' races, how distant these races are from a sensibility of nature and an ability to interpret it, we must recognize that we are in the presence of a singular civilization.

It is important, therefore, in a consideration of the arts in Arabian civilization, to disregard the rather defined idea we have of art itself. By this we mean the expression of intellectual beauty, be it poetic, plastic or musical. Our aesthetic is wholly inappropriate in these concerns, and it would be a mistake to attempt to apply it. Neither should we expect to find in the history of Eastern art an equivalent to the rigorous linkage between different phases that exists in Western art. The Orient is the native soil of all art, as it is of all religion, and the incessant communication between all Asiatics has led to such a diffusion of different manifestations of the activities of these industrious peoples that it is extremely difficult to decipher what is attributable to whom. In all examples of art from the Orient we can trace infinitely diverse influences; we could say that Oriental art is a syncretism of elements such as Byzantine, Persian, Indian, Moorish etc. which combine to form the complex tapestry of Arabic art.

But this is not the place to examine these questions in depth; let us set aside these generalities and approach a subject which is of great importance in Oriental art: interlace, this decorative element, originally invented by the Greeks of the Lower Empire, was adopted by the Orientals who extended and developed it with infinite craft. This process was extremely important: wherever in the world there is evidence of Arab conquests, in India, western Asia, in Africa and Spain, we find this decorative element, and in every edifice it plays such an important role that we could, at least provisionally, consider it as a major characteristic of Arabic art.

Taking the word art in its abstract sense, we could consider Arabic art as a decorative system based entirely on order and geometric form, borrowing little or nothing from the observation of nature; that is to say an art complete in itself, deprived of natural symbolism and idealist significance. The inspiration is abstract and in the execution the plastic has no place. Obviously, this definition is incomplete and too absolute; nevertheless it expresses the truth of the matter well enough. In fact, by its very exaggeration it serves to emphasize the special objective we have in mind, namely an understanding of the importance of geometric information in this decorative art.

There is another important feature of Oriental decorative art, more architectural than decorative, which is also intimately linked with geometry: stalactite columns. Geometric factors figure only marginally in stalactite columns; in a sense they are invisible, featuring only in the design and arrangement of the strata. Of course, from the abstract point of view of science the components of the stalactites are geometric forms, albeit elementary and primitive: but in terms of art these forms are arbitrary; they are subject, as are all architectonic elements, to the strictures of height and also, to some extent, to the will of the artist. There is nothing about them, then, that is definitely and rigorously necessary.

This is certainly not the case so far as interlace is concerned. If we assemble the diverse motifs in order to analyse and compare them, and ultimately to deduce the essential design, we come across a certain number of distinct geometric figures, irreducible one in another, which themselves resolve into simpler and more generous elements and finally to nine elementary polygons, Seen in another way, if we proceed in the inverse sense, taking a specific polygon as the departure point for a decorative motif before the artist's imagination has intervened, we will necessarily obtain a geometric figure derived from this polygon. The interlace design, then, consists of two parts, one essential and one arbitrary. All that is arbitrary stems on the one hand from the artist's imagination and his particular skill and on the other hand from more general influences, allowing for the fact that the decorative art of each territory in the Muslim empire bears its own particular stamp, its own distinct hallmark; the decorative art of Persia is different from Moorish art which is, in turn, distinct from its Egyptian counterpart. This arbitrary factor, therefore, has limitless extensions and it is very likely that our industrial arts will benefit from this new information, turning it to advantage and putting it to new uses.

In all the manual arts there exist a certain number of geometric principles, but these principles are so elementary and so natural that they must be considered as purely instinctive, the common property of all mankind. They are irreducible principles resistant to all analysis. Nevertheless, with the aid of these intuitive principles, at the moment when arts and crafts take on their own definitive identity, we may achieve a certain understanding of geometry, an obscure and undefined science, which, through the perfecting process of industry and the intervention of geometricians, will later arrive at the perfected methods united in that body of doctrine we call descriptive geometry. This may be considered as functional geometry.

But there is another form of geometry, purely formal, which plays a role in industry which is as considerable as that played by functional geometry: this is the geometry we may call aesthetic geometry. At this point, we ask the reader to allow us a digression which is fundamental to our subject and will help towards a fuller understanding of our point of view.

In the West, or in Europe, the progressive evolution of ideas has led to an increasingly marked separation between different types of human activity. This activity, which in its unity of confusion used to be translated in terms of arts and crafts, architecture and fine art, is today governed by method, logic and calculation; as a result of which a compromise has taken place in practice between what is directly related to manual activity, substantive and instinctive, and the intervention of reason which, clearer in nature and subject to higher principles, tends to dominate this activity by imposing on it a structure within which it must now operate.

The ultimate expression of this evolution is to be found in the contemporary organization of industry, where a distinct separation is made between industry *per se* and art and science which have become the object of a singularly perfected culture and which hold sway over manual activity.

Within the arts and sciences we can theoretically distinguish two separate elements: first, that which pertains to 'industry' – the setting to work, with the aid of tools and organization, of materials furnished by nature which human activity exploits and transforms to appropriate them to its needs; second, that which pertains to art in terms of form and decoration. Form is partly the result of conditions particular to any given industry and is partly a function of intention, with the aim of satisfying the innate aesthetic of the artisan. As for decoration, in certain arts it is everything, in others it represents an embellishment of industrial production and gives the totality to its completed form.

In architecture, which is at once an art, a science and an industry, we should distinguish three kinds of elements: first, those pertaining to arts and crafts on which the industry of architecture depends; second, those which pertain to science, that is to say. methodical understanding which is essential to construction and organization and dependent on the mastery of architecture. Form is partly a function of the specific conditions of the industry and science of architecture and partly the result of intention and the aim of satisfying the aesthetic perfection which art demands. Decoration completes the form or is superimposed as an embellishment to buildings in order to satisfy a natural need for luxury and sumptuousness.

Architecture as an art form, when considered in broad perspective, reflects the intellectual life of a people, firstly in the nature and character of the edifices it accords to its institutions and to its forms of worship; then in the figurative, symbolic or talismanic sense it translates the poetic, moral and intellectual ideas of a people through its sculpture and painting.

Since the notion of fine arts is entirely foreign to the modern Orient, it is unnecessary to insist unduly on these observations.

This purely logical analysis is confirmed particularly in modern methods of instruction which industry has already put into practice. It is surely clear that in the mechanical arts, comprising all that pertains to industry in the domain of arts, crafts and architecture, the compromise we mentioned above exists between industry and science through the agency of descriptive geometry, affecting both manual application and pure science. In the industrial arts, this compromise functions between art and industry by means of the art of design, which on the one hand borders on manual application and on the other is elevated to the level of inspiration necessitated by the fine arts.

Thus, all that pertains to industry in arts, crafts and architecture includes the application of functional geometry as exposed in the treatises of elementary and descriptive geometry. This functional geometry also plays a part in the purely technical aspect of the art of design.

That which pertains to art in the realm of arts and crafts, and of architecture, that is to say essentially in form and decoration, depends upon an entirely different geometry which we may term aesthetic geometry with which all artisans are familiar, at least on the level of sentiment if not on the level of science.

We should not understand by this that art is subordinate to geometry – that would be absurd, or at least true only in a metaphysical sense – but we should understand that aesthetic geometry, providing the theory of forms, essentially includes all that pertains to order and form as viewed in their purely abstract sense. To reiterate, this means that aesthetic geometry, in evidence as much in art as in nature, attains the stature of a real art form, as it serves to translate by means of geometric figures the precise conditions of order, proportion and harmony which make up the specific nature of form in any given artistic endeavour.

Aesthetic geometry cannot be the object of a science or any didactic exposition so long as we restrict ourselves to the elementary factors of pure intuition which serve the purposes of art. But these are the factors which, basically, constitute defined geometric figures, and the object of aesthetic geometry is the theory of these geometric figures, each defined by its own generic character.

In the arts of the Orient since Islam, aesthetic geometry has been the principal element of inspiration in what concerns form and decoration. This geometry has taken the place, so to speak, of the concept of nature in the plastic sense which is inexistent among the semitic or semiticized races. The study of Arabic art is therefore particularly interesting in that it reveals the most considerable application of geometric forms to monumental and decorative arts ever realized.

In decoration the Orientals specifically made use of various forms of polygonal figures, skilfully modifying them to their own needs and to the caprices of their own vision. By linking together successive patterns as a result of the application of theoretical principles they created the interlace decoration which is to be found in profusion in all their buildings, chiselled into stone and bronze, carved into the joints of their woodwork, hollowed into the plaster for revetments and windows, painted on the faïence tiles – a wholly original decorative form.

The application of these principles essentially constitutes what we mean by the 'line' in Arabic art. Now this application is entirely subordinate to the skill of the artisan and in no way supposes reasoned, scientific knowledge of geometry. In fact, we should not imagine that the Orientals, in the period when they constructed the buildings, had a well-defined theory on which to base their richly varied invention. The Arabs made use of geometry without any real understanding of the science of geometry and when they invented stalactite vaulting and interlace this was not the deduction of a hitherto unknown theory but – and this is particular to their art – the simultaneous perception of pure form and of the work to be accomplished.

Art, unlike science, does not require a rigorous enumeration and definition of its component parts. Art sets in motion the creation of a spectacle for the eyes; whether the basic elements are great or small in number is unimportant, everything depends on decisions made by the architect concerning the means at his disposal. In this way, the geometric bases in Moorish interlace can be reduced to two principal forms: the square and its derivative figures, and the hexagon and its derivatives.

Jules Bourgoin
1873

THE PLATES

PLATE 1

MOSQUE OF TALĀ´Ī` IBN RUZZĪK

Details of stucco and woodwork

TWELFTH CENTURY

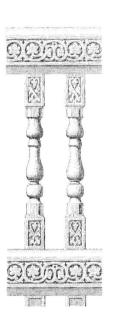

PLATE 2

Columns and pillars

NINTH–FIFTEENTH CENTURIES

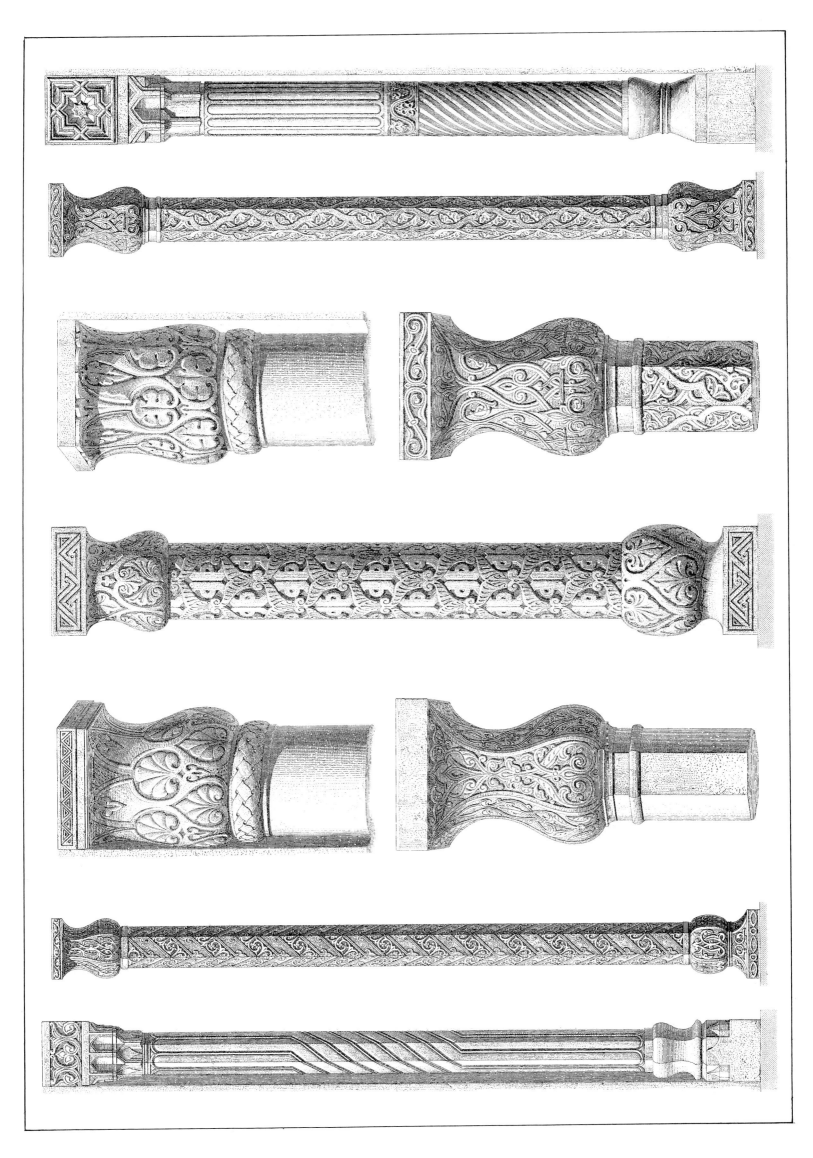

PLATE 3

MOSQUE OF QAWSŪN

Window decoration

FOURTEENTH CENTURY

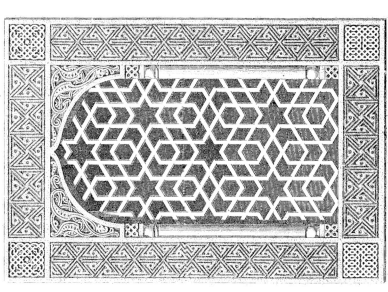

PLATE 4

MOSQUE OF ṬALĀ´I` IBN RUZZĪK

Main door

TWELFTH CENTURY

PLATE 5

MASHRABIYYAH

Carved wooden screens

PLATE 6

Mashrabiyyah

Turned wooden screens

PLATE 7

Mashrabiyyah

Turned wooden screens

PLATE 8

MASHRABIYYAH

Wooden screens

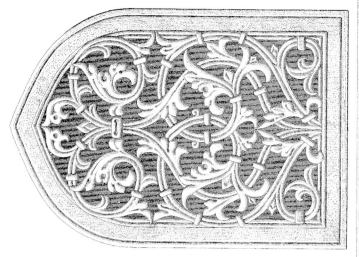
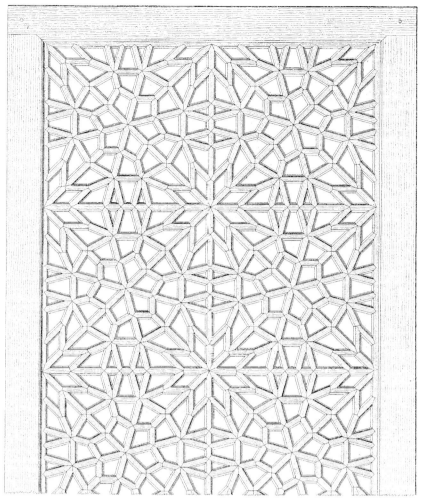

PLATE 9

Mashrabiyyah

Wooden screens

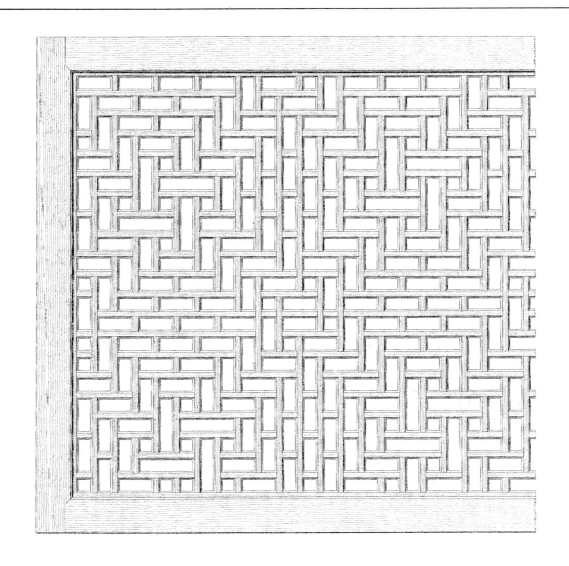

PLATE 10

Tekke cheikh haçen sadaka

Detail of decoration on the dome

FOURTEENTH CENTURY

PLATE 11

MADRASAH (COLLEGE) OF AMIR SUNQUR SA'DI (SHAYKH ḤASAN ṢADAQAH)

Detail of decoration on the dome

FOURTEENTH CENTURY

MADRASAH (COLLEGE) OF AMIR SUNQUR SA'DI (SHAYKH ḤASAN ṢADAQAH)

Detail of decoration on the dome

FOURTEENTH CENTURY

PLATE 12

Wall mosaics

TWELFTH AND FOURTEENTH CENTURY

PLATE 13

TOMB OF SULTAN BARSBĀY (EAST CEMETERY)

Mosaic panelling

FIFTEENTH CENTURY

PLATE 14

TOMB OF SULTAN BARSBĀY (EAST CEMETERY)

Mosaic panelling

FIFTEENTH CENTURY

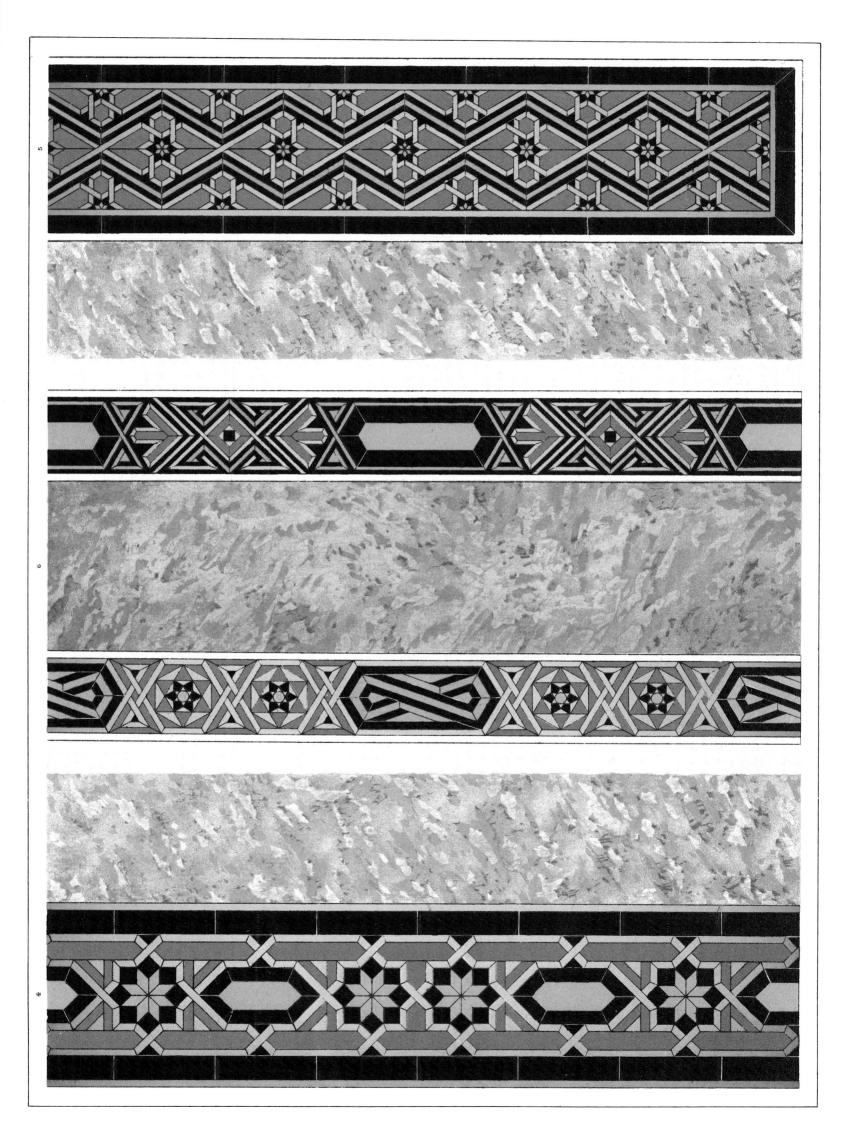

PLATE 15

Wall mosaics

FIFTEENTH AND SIXTEENTH CENTURY

PLATE 16

Floor mosaics and tiling

SIXTEENTH CENTURY

PLATE 19

MOSQUE OF AL-BURDAYNĪ

Interior

LATE SEVENTEENTH CENTURY

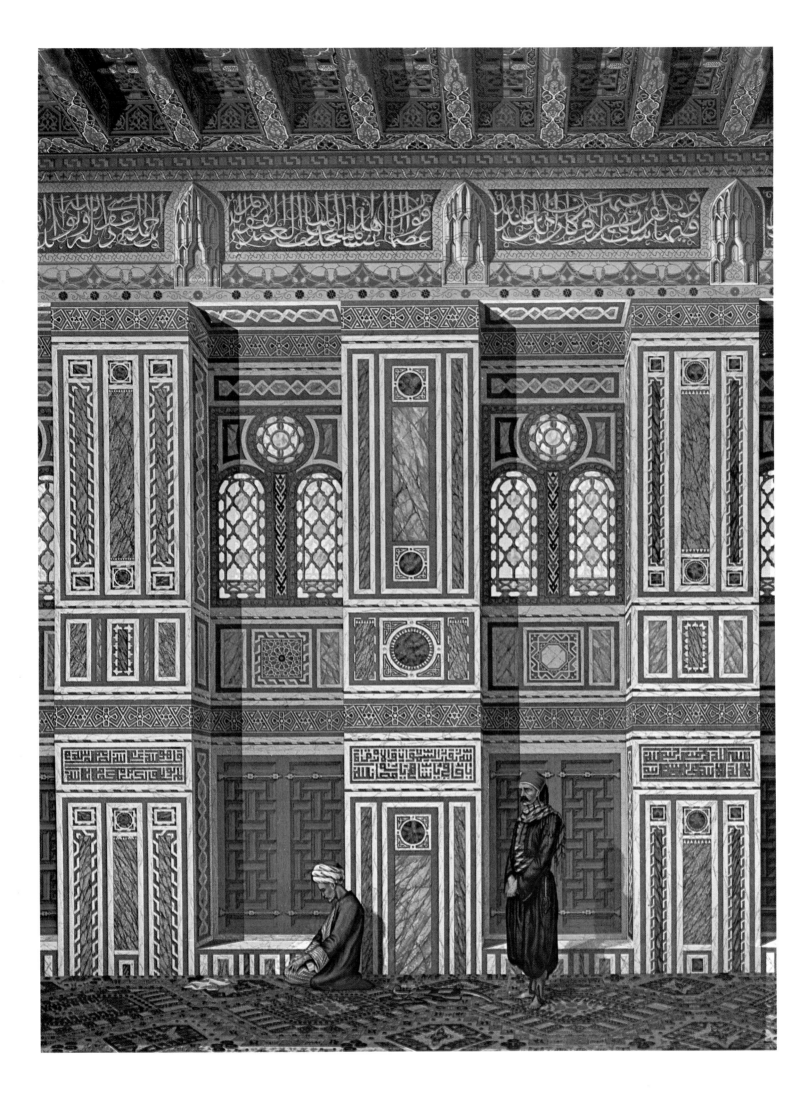

PLATE 20

MOSQUE OF AL-BURDAYNĪ

Wall mosaics

LATE SEVENTEENTH CENTURY

PLATE 21
Mosque of al-burdaynī

Wall mosaics

LATE SEVENTEENTH CENTURY

PLATE 22

Mosque of al-Burdaynī

Mosaic on the miḥrāb

LATE SEVENTEENTH CENTURY

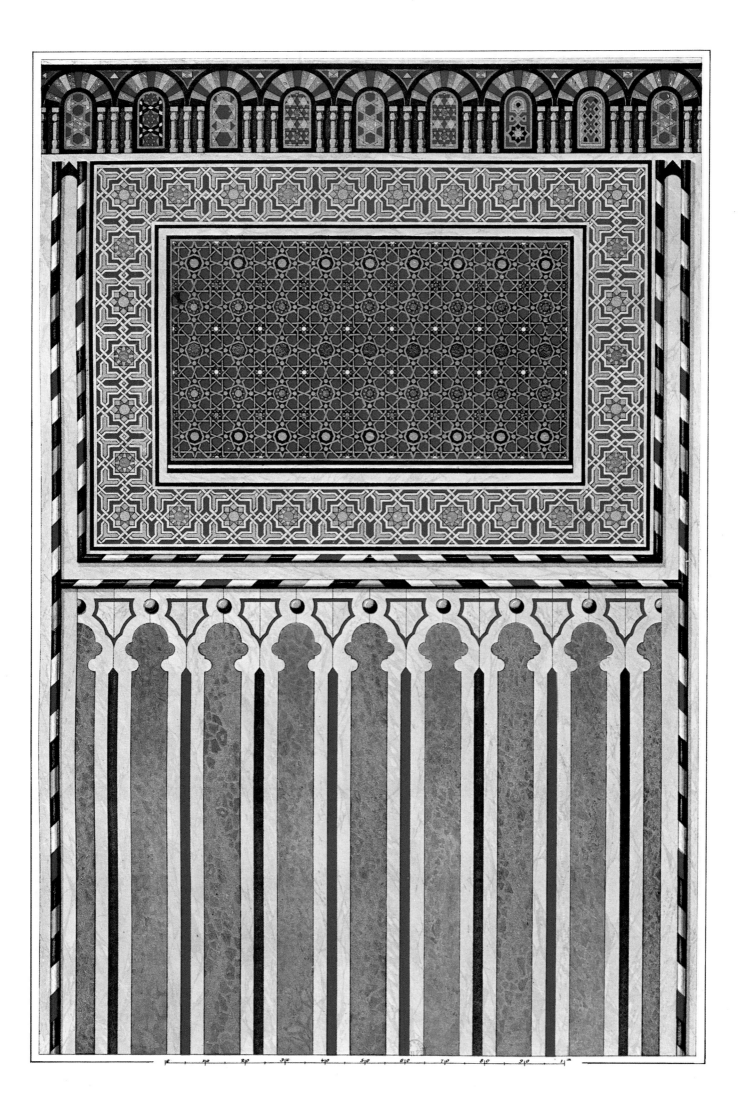

PLATE 23

Mosque of al-Burdaynī

Mosaic on the miḥrāb

LATE SEVENTEENTH CENTURY

PLATE 24

MOSQUE OF QAWĀM AL-DĪN

Marble friezes and rosette

EIGHTEENTH CENTURY

PLATE 25

MOSQUE OF AL-BURDAYNĪ

Ceiling and frieze from the dikkah (platform)

LATE SEVENTEENTH CENTURY

PLATE 26

MOSQUE OF AL-BURDAYNĪ

Main ceiling (detail)

LATE SEVENTEENTH CENTURY

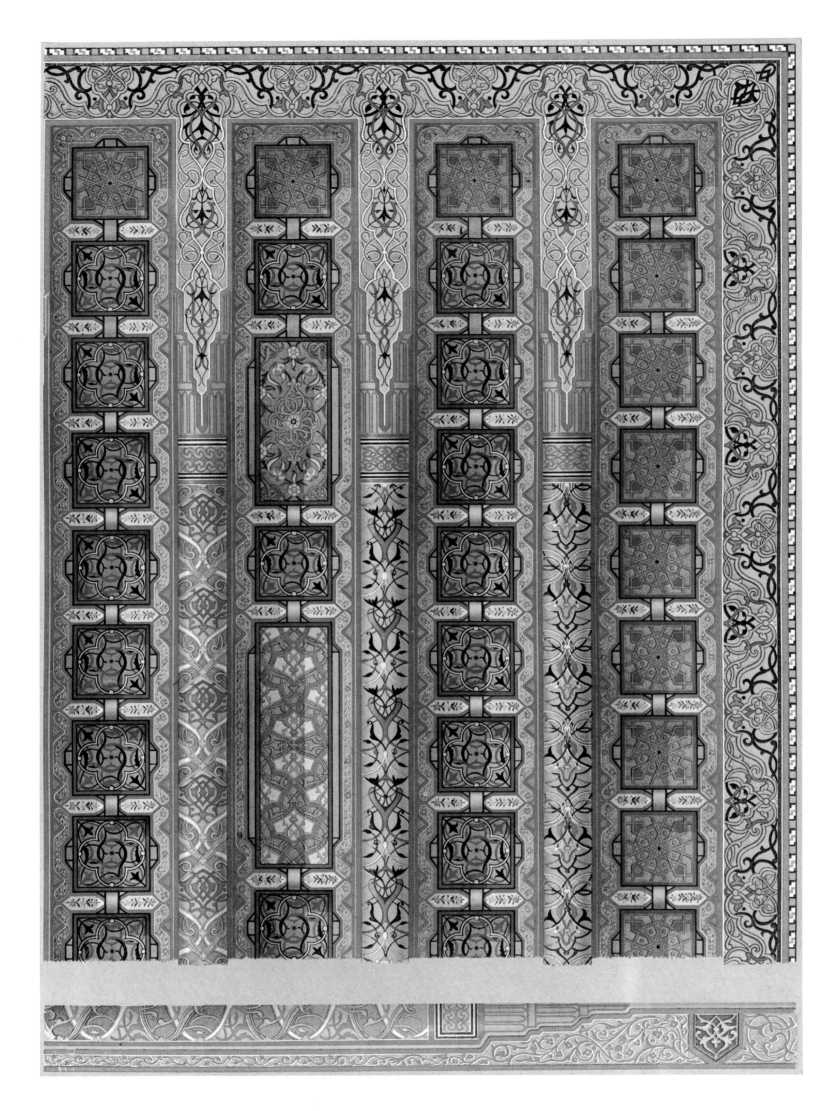

PLATE 27

MOSQUE OF AL-BURDAYNĪ

Main ceiling (detail)

LATE SEVENTEENTH CENTURY

PLATE 28

Mosque of al-burdaynī

Friezes and border decorations from the smaller rooms

LATE SEVENTEENTH CENTURY

PLATE 29

MOSQUE OF AL-BURDAYNĪ

Ceiling decoration – interlace patterns

LATE SEVENTEENTH CENTURY

PLATE 30

MOSQUE OF AL-BURDAYNĪ

Ceiling decoration – interlace patterns

LATE SEVENTEENTH CENTURY

PLATE 31

MOSQUE OF AL-BURDAYNĪ

Ceiling decoration – interlace patterns

LATE SEVENTEENTH CENTURY

PLATE 32

THE BAYT (HOUSE) AL-SHALABY

Ceiling decoration

EIGHTEENTH CENTURY

PLATE 33

The bayt (house) al-shalabī

Ceiling decoration

EIGHTEENTH CENTURY

PLATE 34

THE BAYT (HOUSE) AL-SHALABĪ

Ceiling decoration

EIGHTEENTH CENTURY

PLATE 35

Ceiling decoration

EIGHTEENTH CENTURY

PLATE 36

Ceiling decoration – arrangement of starred dodecagons

PLATE 37

Ceiling decoration – arrangement of starred octagons

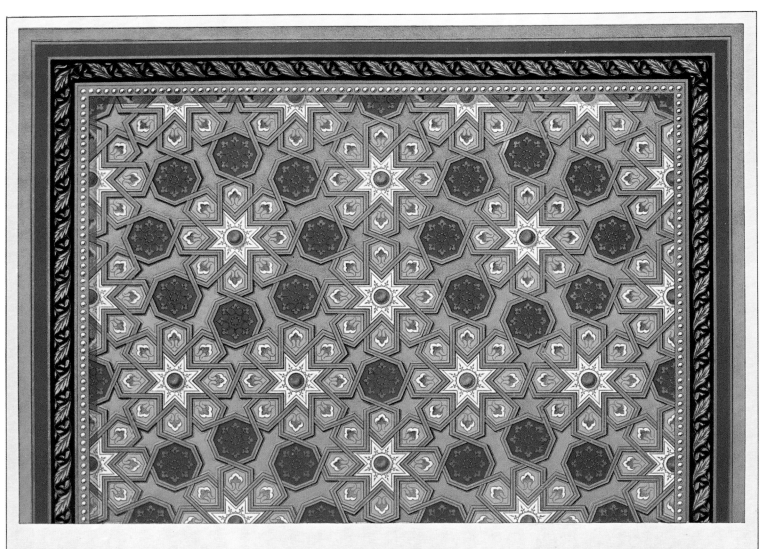

PLATE 38

Ceiling decoration – arrangement of starred octagons

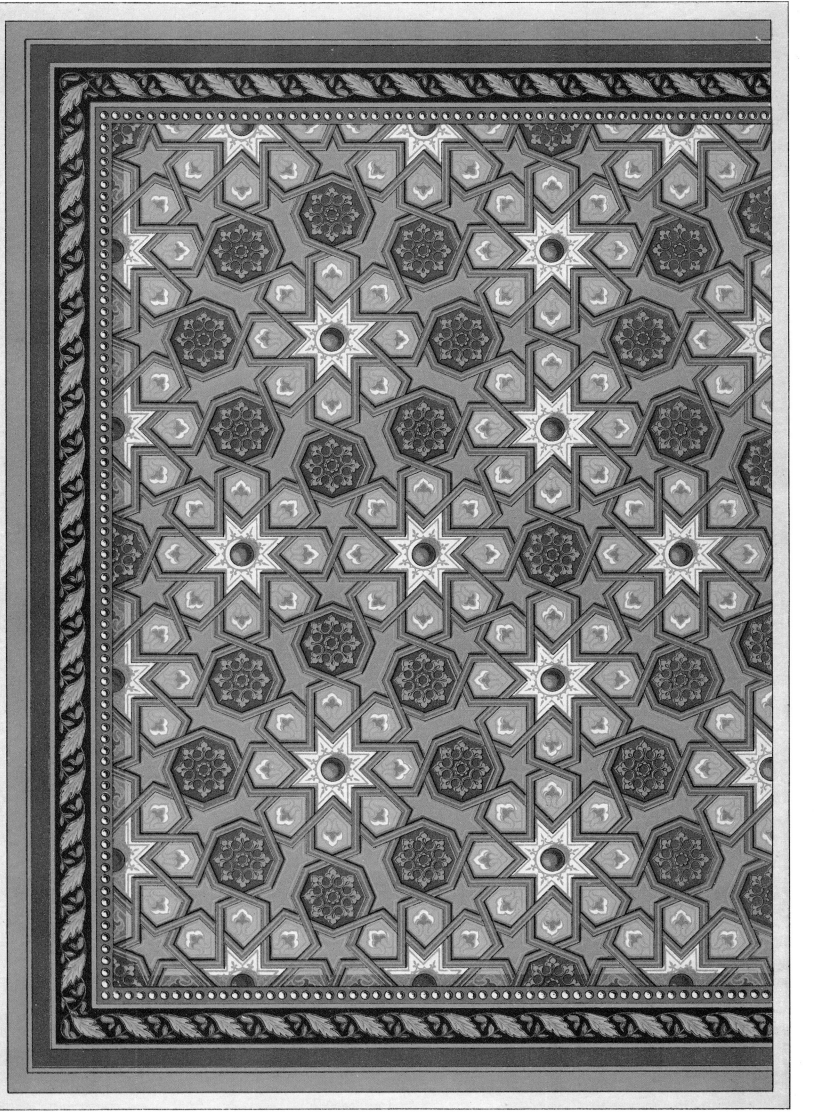

PLATE 39

Ceiling decoration – arrangement of starred octagons

PLATE 40

GREAT MOSQUE AT QŪS

Door of the minbar (detail)

TWELFTH CENTURY

PLATE 42

Maristān (hospital) of sultan qalāwūn

Fatimid wooden panels

TWELFTH CENTURY

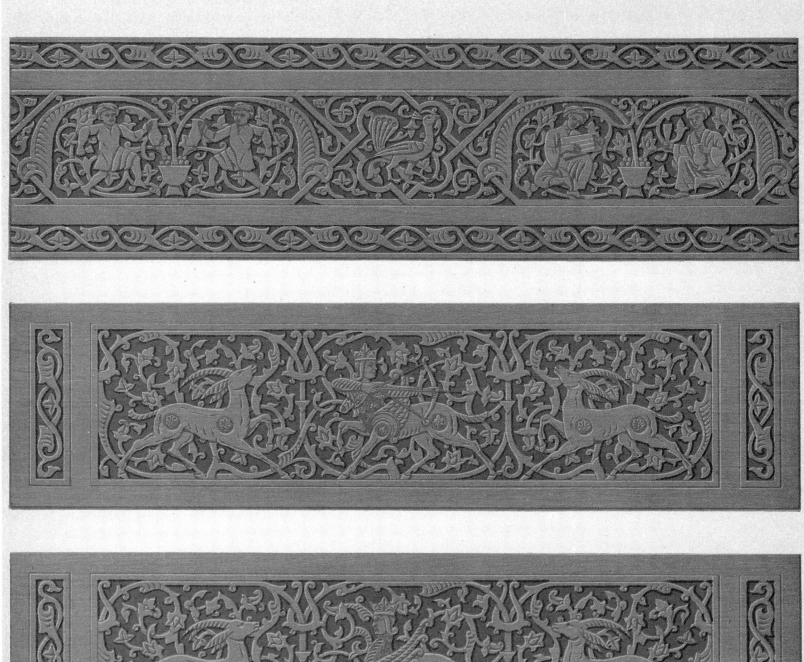

PLATE 43

Mosque of sultan qayt-bay (al-kabsh)

Elevations of the minbar

FIFTEENTH CENTURY

PLATE 44

TOMB OF SULTAN QANṢŪḤ AL-GHAWRĪ

Cupboard doors and borders in carved wood

SIXTEENTH CENTURY

PLATE 45

Wooden partitions and borders

PLATE 46

Mosque of amir ālwās

Main exterior door

FOURTEENTH CENTURY

PLATE 47

Mosque of sultan Qáyt-bāy

Ornamentation of doors and cupboards

LATE FIFTEENTH CENTURY

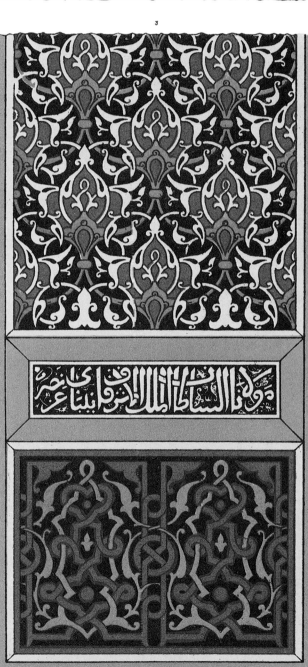

PLATE 48

DETAILS OF A DOOR FROM A MOSQUE AT AL-KHANKAH

EIGHTEENTH CENTURY

DETAILS OF A DOOR FROM A MOSQUE AT AL-KHANKAH

EIGHTEENTH CENTURY

PLATE 49

MIḤRĀB FROM THE MOSQUE OF SHAYKHU

Wall tiling

PLATE 50

W ALL TILING

Decorative borders

SIXTEENTH CENTURY

PLATE 51

Palace of khurshid pasha (destroyed)

Tile panel representing the Ka`bah and its surroundings

SIXTEENTH CENTURY

PALACE OF KHURSHID PASHA (DESTROYED)

Tile panel representing the Ka`bah and its surroundings

SIXTEENTH CENTURY

PLATE 52

A PAVILION

Wall tiling

SIXTEENTH CENTURY

PLATE 53

PAVILION OF MĀHŪBAY

Wall tiling

SIXTEENTH CENTURY

PLATE 54

GREAT MOSQUE AT QŪS

Ceramic tympanum and spandrels

SIXTEENTH CENTURY

PLATE 55

PALACE OF ISMĀ`ĪL BĀY (DESTROYED)

Wall tiling

SIXTEENTH CENTURY

PALACE OF ISMĀ`ĪL BĀY (DESTROYED)

Wall tiling

SIXTEENTH CENTURY

PLATE 56

QAṢR RAḌWĀN

Wall tiling

SEVENTEENTH CENTURY

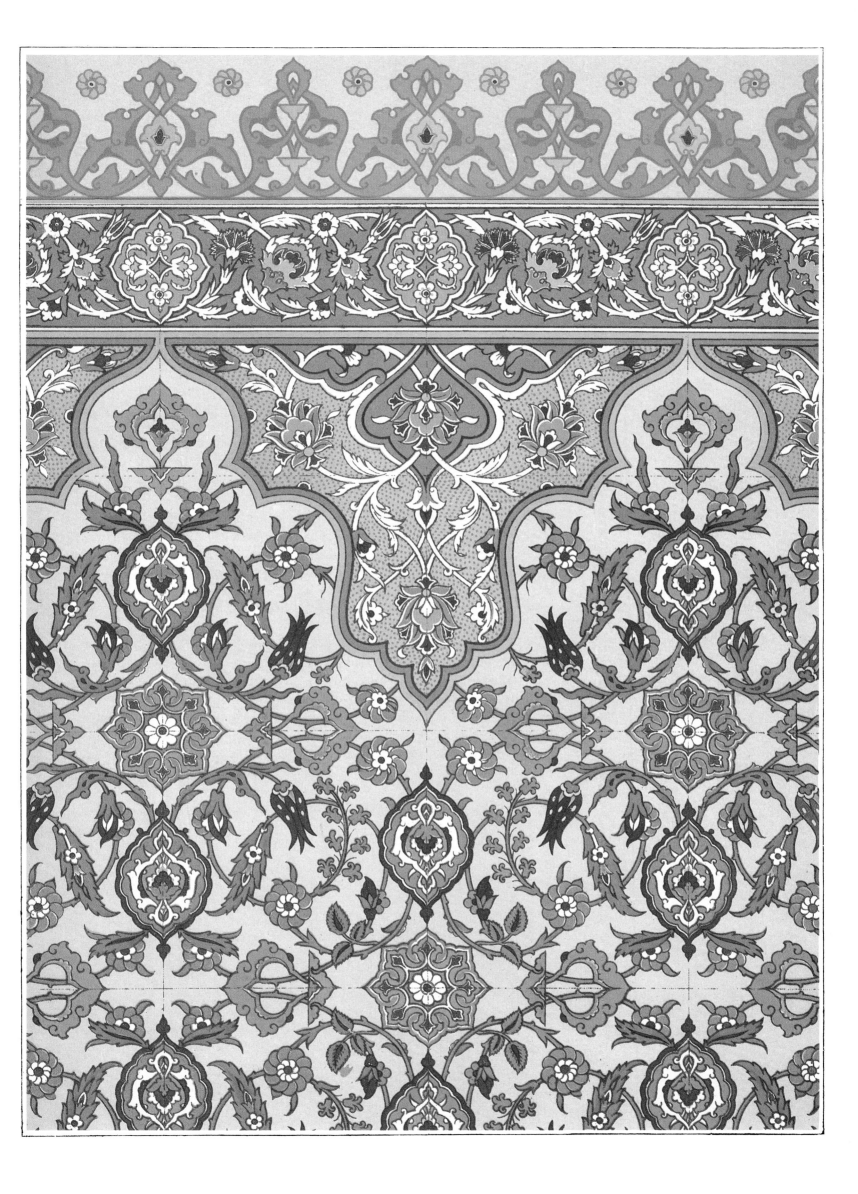

PLATE 57

Qaṣr Raḍwān

Wall tiling

SEVENTEENTH CENTURY

PLATE 58

Mosque of amir aqsunqur (ibrāhīm aghā)

Ceramic tile panel

SEVENTEENTH CENTURY

Mosque of amir aqsunqur (ibrāhīm aghā)

Ceramic tile panel

SEVENTEENTH CENTURY

PLATE 59

DERVISH TEKKE

Wall tiling

SEVENTEENTH CENTURY

PLATE 60

DERVISH TEKKE

Tympanum and border of an arcade – enamelled pottery

PLATE 61

BAYT (HOUSE) AL-AMIR

Wall tiling

SEVENTEENTH CENTURY

PLATE 62

Wall tiling

EIGHTEENTH CENTURY

PLATE 63

Mosque of amīr shaykhū

Wall tiling

EIGHTEENTH CENTURY

PLATE 64

FOUNTAIN OF ABD AL-RAḤMĀN KATKHUDĀ GAMĀLIYYAH

Wall tiling

EIGHTEENTH CENTURY

FOUNTAIN OF ABD AL-RAḤMĀN KATKHUDĀ GAMĀLIYYAH

Wall tiling

EIGHTEENTH CENTURY

PLATE 65

Studies of leaves and flowers – painted pottery

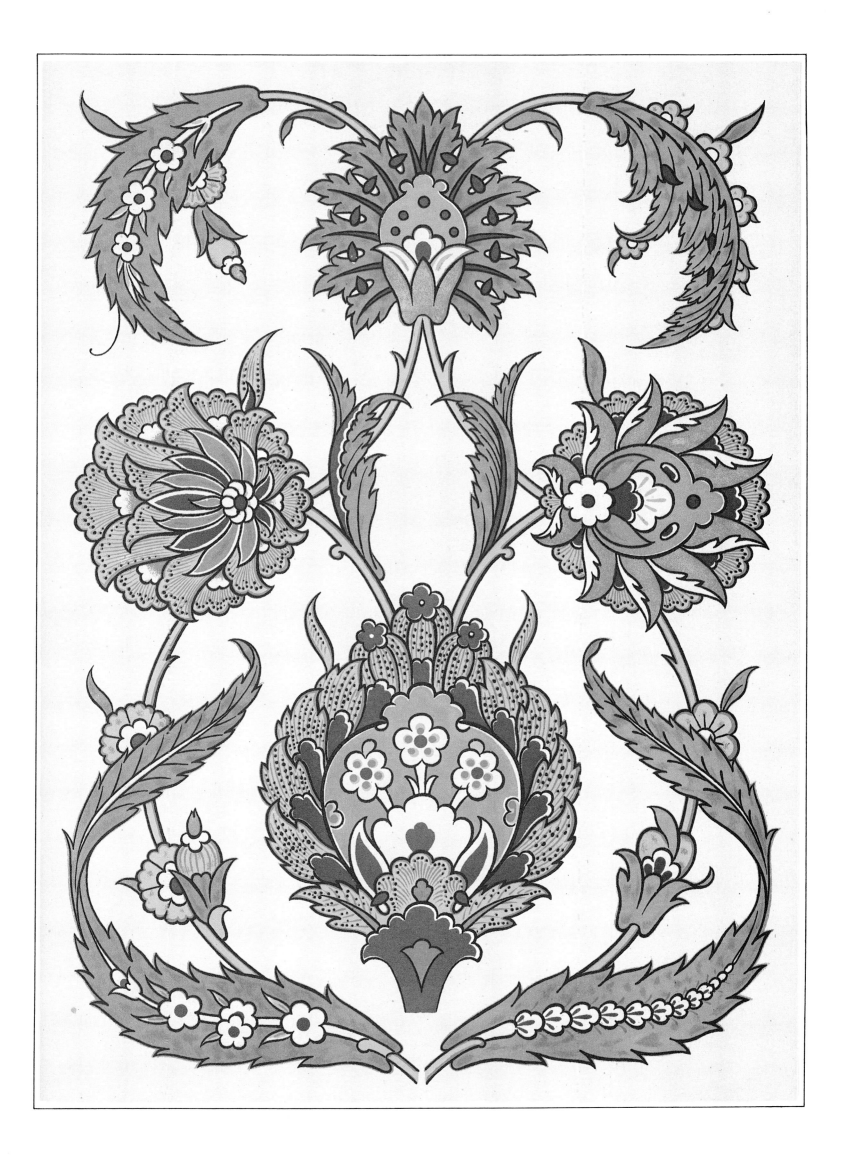

PLATE 66

Ceramic panel

PLATE 67

Ḥanūt (mortuary)

Wall tiling

PLATE 68

Ḥanūt (mortuary)

Wall tiling

PLATE 69

MOSQUE OF SULAYMĀN PASHȦ (SIDI SĀRIYAH)

Decoration above the door of the minbar

EIGHTEENTH CENTURY

PLATE 70

THE HOUSE OF SĪDĪ YŪSUF ADĀMĪ

Upper room

PLATE 71

THE HOUSE OF SĪDĪ YŪSUF ADĀMĪ

The nurse's room

PLATE 72

House of husnī aḥmad al-burdayni (destroyed)

qa'ah (salon)

SEVENTEENTH CENTURY

House of husnī aḥmad al-burdayni (destroyed)

qa'ah (salon)

SEVENTEENTH CENTURY

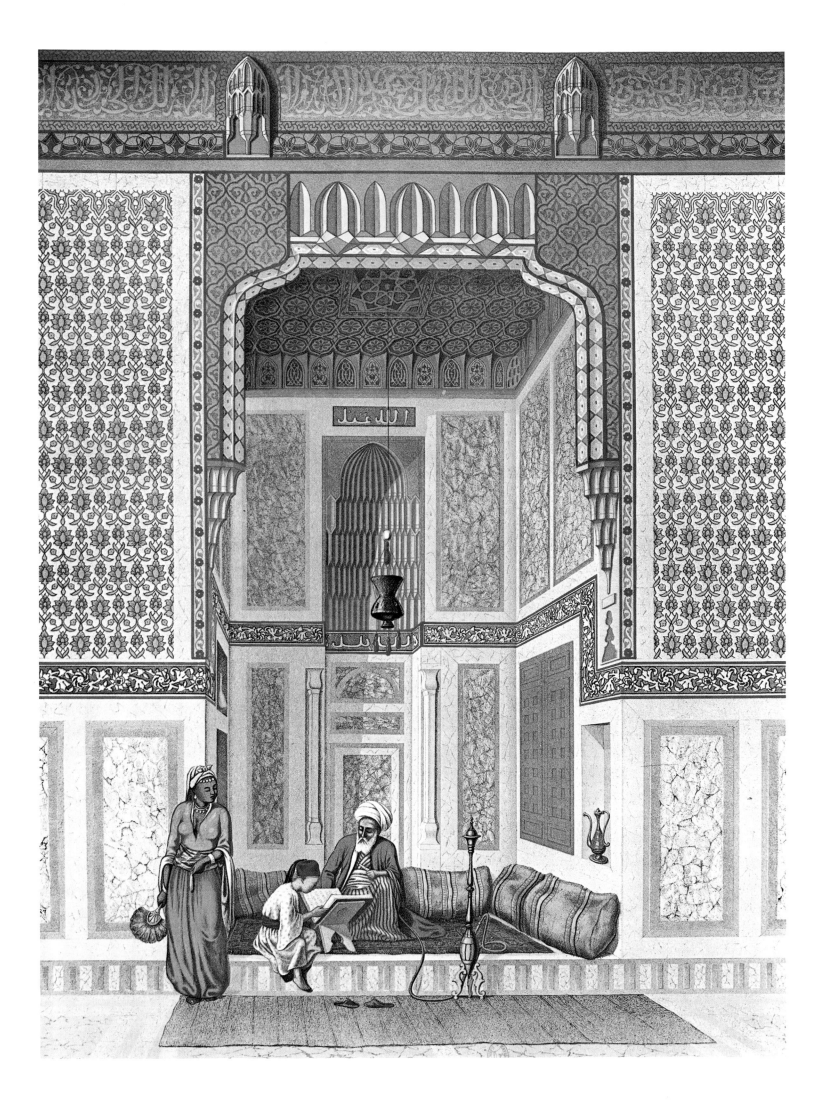

PLATE 73

Mosque of sultan barqūq

Decorated bottle

LATE FOURTEENTH CENTURY

PLATE 74

MADRASAH (COLLEGE) OF SULTAN BARSBĀY

Shamsiyyah (Stained-glass window)

PLATE 75

Wall-hanging

TWELFTH CENTURY

PLATE 76

CHURCH AT NIVELLES

Patterned textile

FOURTEENTH CENTURY

PLATE 77

Small ornamental carpet

FOURTEENTH CENTURY

PLATE 79

QUIVER AND BOW

Pierced leather over velvet

SIXTEENTH CENTURY

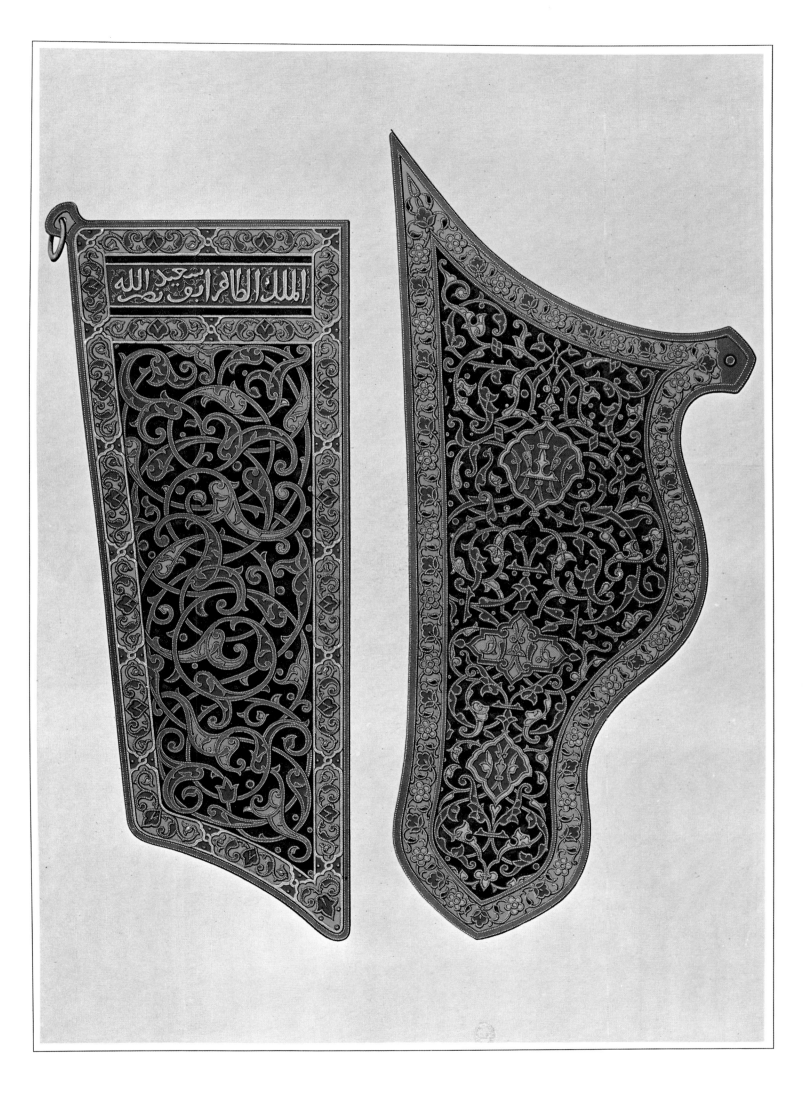

PLATE 80

Large ornamental carpet

EIGHTEENTH CENTURY

PLATE 81

Ḥayṭah — (Wall hanging)

EIGHTEENTH CENTURY

Ḥayṭah — (Wall hanging)

EIGHTEENTH CENTURY

PLATE 82

Armour of sultan tūmāb-bāy ii

Steel inlaid with silver and gold

EARLY SIXTEENTH CENTURY

PLATE 83

Damascened bronze tray

PLATE 84

CANDLESTICK AND TRAY BELONGING TO SULTAN AL-NĀṢIR MUḤAMMAD

EARLY FOURTEENTH CENTURY

PLATE 85

Writing case of sultan sha`bān ii

Brass inlaid with silver and gold

MID-FOURTEENTH CENTURY

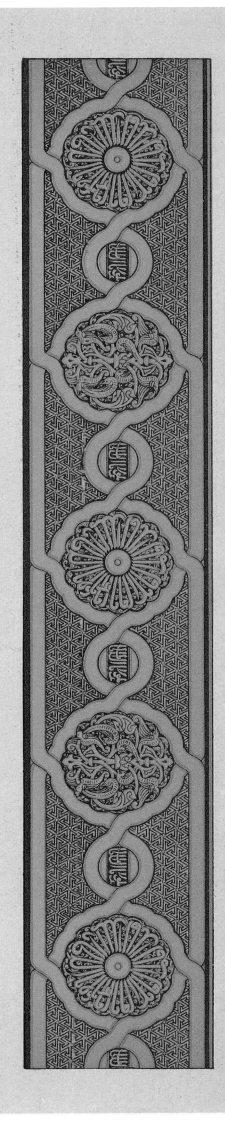

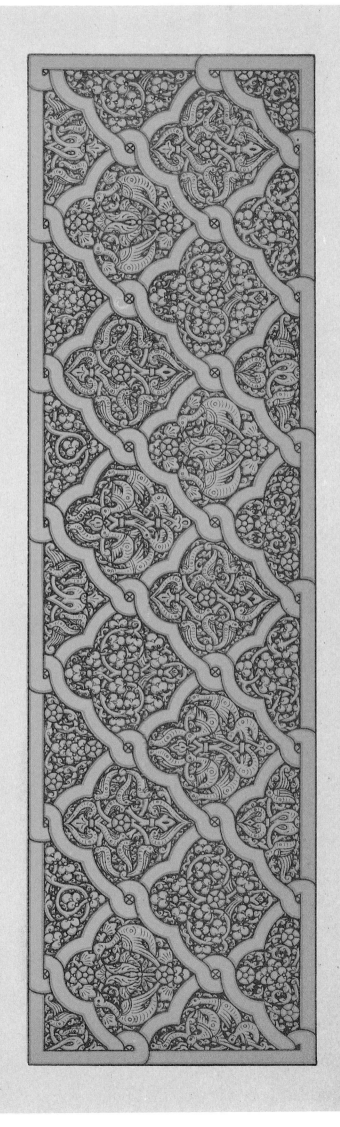

PLATE 87

BINDINGS

SIXTEENTH CENTURY

PLATE 88

CUT PAPER WORK

LATE EIGHTEENTH CENTURY

PLATE 89

CUT PAPER WORK

LATE EIGHTEENTH CENTURY

PLATE 90

MAQĀMĀT (ASSEMBLIES) OF ḤARĪRĪ

Frontispiece

THIRTEENTH CENTURY

PLATE 91

MAQĀMĀT (ASSEMBLIES) OF ḤARĪRĪ

THIRTEENTH CENTURY

PLATE 92

Maqāmāt (assemblies) of Ḥarīrī

A pavilion

THIRTEENTH CENTURY

PLATE 93

Maqāmāt (assemblies) of Ḥarīrī

A caravan

THIRTEENTH CENTURY

وَسَكَنِي وَمَسْكَنِي وَحَوْلِي وَجَاهِي وَمَآبِي وَمَالِي وَلَا تُلْقِنِي لِنَفْسِي وَلَا

تُسَلِّطْ عَلَىَّ مُغِيرًا وَاجْعَلْ لِي مِنْ لَدُنْكَ سُلْطَانًا نَصِيرًا اللَّهُمَّ اجْرُشْنِي بِعَيْنِكَ وَعَوْنِكَ

وَاحْفَظْنِي بِأَمْنِكَ وَمِنَّكَ وَتَوَلَّنِي بِاخْتِيَارِكَ وَخِبْرِكَ وَلَا تَكِلْنِي إِلَى كِلَاءَةِ غَيْرِكَ

وَهَبْ لِي عَافِيَةً غَيْرَ عَافِيَةٍ وَارْزُقْنِي رَفَاهِيَةً غَيْرَ وَاهِيَةٍ وَأَغْنِنِي بِجَاهِي اللَّاوَآءَ

PLATE 94

MOSQUE OF QAWSŪN

Page from a Koran

FOURTEENTH CENTURY

PLATE 95

Mosque of sultan barqūq

Page from a Koran

LATE FOURTEENTH CENTURY

PLATE 96

TOMB OF SULTAN QĀNṢŪḤ AL-GHAWRĪ

Ornamentation of a Koran

EARLY SIXTEENTH CENTURY

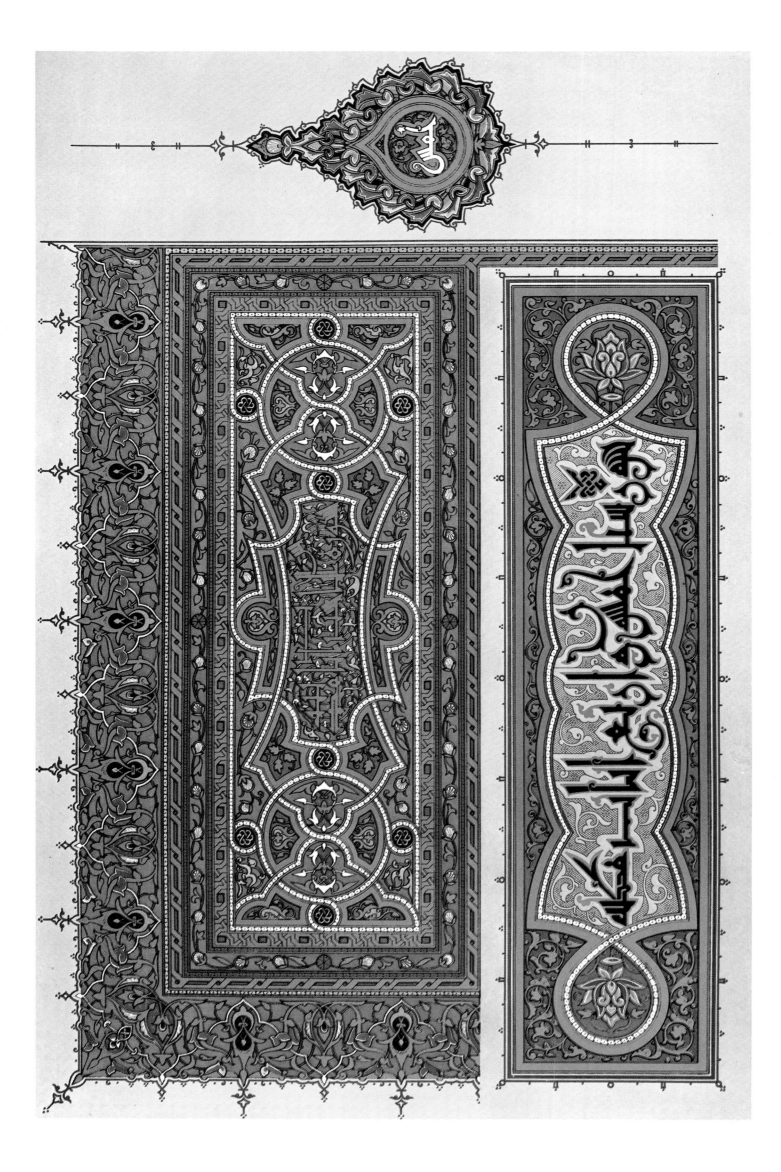

PLATE 97

TOMB OF SULTAN QĀNṢŪḤ AL-GHAWRĪ

Ornamentation of a Koran

EARLY SIXTEENTH CENTURY

PLATE 98

TOMB OF SULTAN QĀNṢŪḤ AL-GHAWRĪ

Ornamentation of a Koran

EARLY SIXTEENTH CENTURY

PLATE 99

Tomb of sultan qānṣūḥ al-ghawrī

Ornamentation of a Koran

SIXTEENTH CENTURY

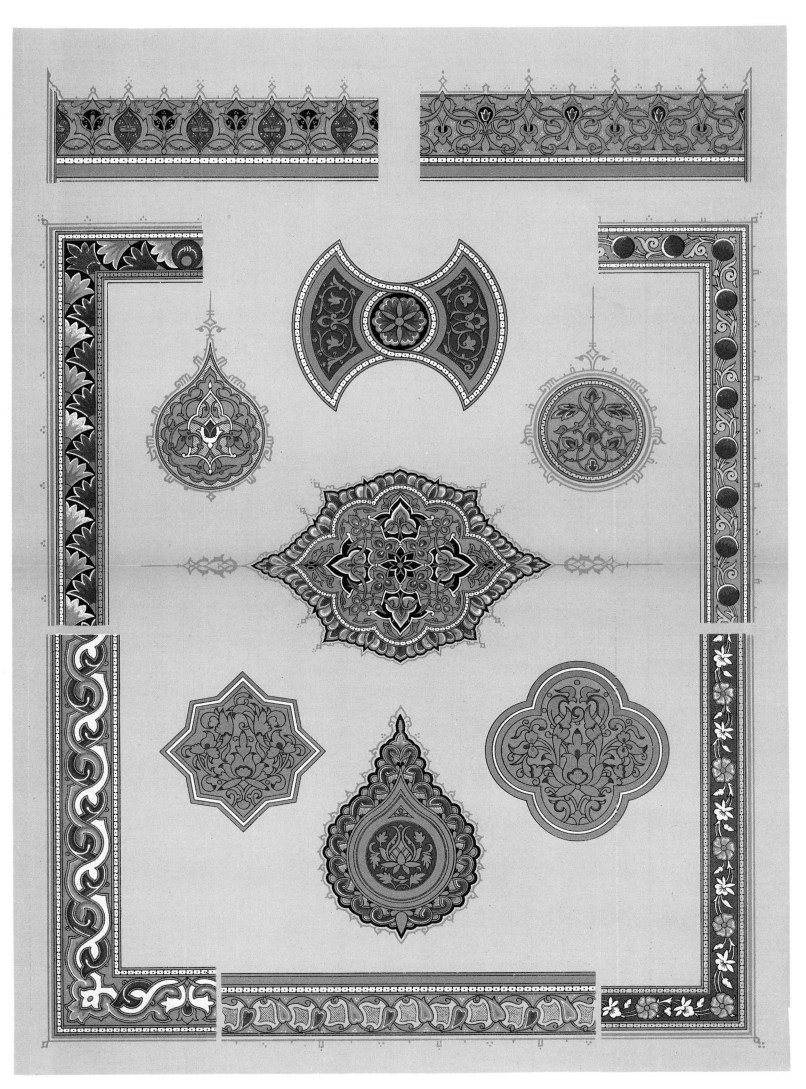

PLATE 100

Page from an arabic manuscript

SIXTEENTH CENTURY

PLATE 101

Frontispiece and detail from a Koran

SEVENTEENTH CENTURY

PLATE 102

Ornamentation of a Koran
SEVENTEENTH CENTURY

من كلام الله تعالى

ما في قلوبهم في الأرض

وعظهم وقل لهم في أنفسهم قولاً بليغاً وما أرسلنا من رسول إلا ليطاع بإذن الله ولو أنهم إذ ظلموا أنفسهم جاؤوك فاستغفروا الله واستغفر لهم

الرسول لوجدوا الله

من كلام الله تعالى

PLATE 103

FACING PAGES FROM A KORAN BELONGING TO SULTAN MOḤAMMAD III OF

MOROCCO

EIGHTEENTH CENTURY

FACING PAGES FROM A KORAN BELONGING TO SULTAN MOḤAMMAD III OF

MOROCCO

EIGHTEENTH CENTURY

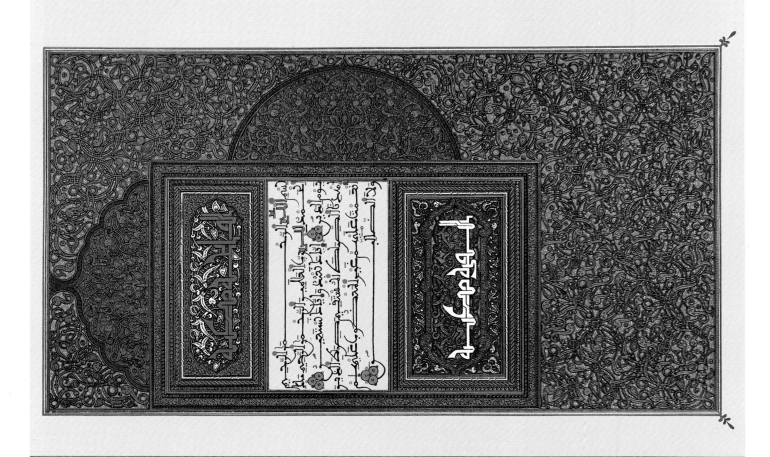

PLATE 104

FACING PAGES FROM A KORAN BELONGING TO SULTAN MOḤAMMAD III OF

MOROCCO

EIGHTEENTH CENTURY

PLATE 105

FACING PAGES FROM A KORAN BELONGING TO SULTAN MOḤAMMAD III OF

MOROCCO

EIGHTEENTH CENTURY

FACING PAGES FROM A KORAN BELONGING TO SULTAN MOḤAMMAD III OF

MOROCCO

EIGHTEENTH CENTURY

PLATE 106

PAGE FROM A KORAN BELONGING TO SULTAN MOḤAMMAD III OF MOROCCO
EIGHTEENTH CENTURY

PAGE FROM A KORAN BELONGING TO SULTAN MOḤAMMAD III OF MOROCCO
EIGHTEENTH CENTURY

PLATE 107

PAGE FROM A KORAN BELONGING TO SULTAN MOḤAMMAD III OF MOROCCO
EIGHTEENTH CENTURY

PLATE 108

ORNAMENTATION OF A KORAN BELONGING TO SULTAN MOḤAMMAD III OF

MOROCCO

EIGHTEENTH CENTURY

PLATE 109

ORNAMENTATION OF A KORAN BELONGING TO SULTAN MOḤAMMAD III OF

MOROCCO

EIGHTEENTH CENTURY